The Power of ^{2}

Exponential Sales Leadership

The Power of ^{2}

Exponential Sales Leadership

Jamie Crosbie and Jay Blakey

2015

The Power of ^{2}: Exponential Sales Leadership

First Printing: 2015

ISBN 978-0-692-56269-7

ProActivate, LLC
1560 E. Southlake Blvd. Suite 231
Southlake, TX 76092

www.ProActivate.net

Contents

Acknowledgements v

Foreword...vii

Chapter 1: The Challenges of Today's Sales Organization 3

Chapter 2: Organizational Leadership (Pros and Cons) 14

Chapter 3: Introducing the Engaged Sales Management
Squared Method (ESM²) 27

Chapter 4: (ESM²) Benefits to the Sales Staff 37

Chapter 5: Benefits to the Prospect/ Client................................45

Chapter 6: Benefits to the Sales Organization 50

Chapter 7: Things to do to Convert to ESM² 57

About ProActivate 67

References 68

Acknowledgements

The authors would like to acknowledge Victoria Cayce with great appreciation and gratitude for her assistance in writing this book.

Legal Disclaimer

Foreword

The word "engaged" comes from the French word "engager" meaning a promise to get married, it seems like a good metaphor for describing the relationship between the sales manager and salespeople. Another way to look at this relationship through the lens of engagement is to look inside. My view is that our outer environment is a reflection of our inner mindset. Your conversations with your salespeople are always a reflection of the conversations you have inside your mind. The big question you want to ask yourself: are you aware of your Mindset Operating System?

Your mindset is a set of attitudes and beliefs that influence and shape your behaviors. According to scientific research, we start to create these attitudes and beliefs the moment we're born. You store them in a particular area of your brain, called the prefrontal cortex. This is where neural connections form into cognitive elements, memories, and associated feelings from past experiences. Some call this the executive function of the brain -- I like to think of the prefrontal cortex as our "inner CEO."

Do you have a strong inner CEO? When your mindset is functioning at optimum levels, you're better able to excel in tough sales management situations. That's because high achievers consciously create a belief system that helps them cope effectively with difficult situations at work. This is according to scientific research conducted by Professor Michael Bernard at the University of Melbourne, Australia.

I've had the good fortune in my professional life to interview two great motivators: Zig Ziglar and Tony Robbins. They both passed on wisdom that has stuck with me. Zig Ziglar said, "Success is not measured by what you have done compared to others, but compared to what you're capable of doing." Tony Robbins said, "Everything you need to succeed is within us now."

Although motivation is important in sales and in management, motivation alone is not enough. Great sales leaders know that motivational rhetoric has to be backed by resilience. I learned this insight from Dr. Abraham Zaleznik, a professor at Harvard Business School who said, "Success is not the result of focusing on success, but how we handle the disappointments that are inevitable in the evolution of our careers." In other words, engaged sales managers lead with empathy and they offer support when salespeople suffer a setback. Setbacks are nothing but invitations for a comeback. If you belief system includes the idea that disappointments are the cradle of ambition, then your behavioral strengths will win over any adversity.

Dr. Paul Stoltz wrote in his book "Grit" that we experience 23 adversities on an average day. In sales, we may experience 40 or more. Successful leaders welcome adversity as a stepping stone, or they view it as the diamond dust that nature uses to polish its jewels.

Just today I had a conversation with a salesman who sat on flight US 1549 that was piloted by "Sully" Sullenberger and crash landed after takeoff from LaGuardia airport in the Hudson River. The sales rep sat in First Class, looking out the window at takeoff when geese hit both engines of the A320 airbus. He described the noise; "as if you tossed sneakers into a washing machine" the grinding noise got louder and within a few seconds both engines stopped and the plane began to lose altitude. Sullenberger who was also trained as a glider pilot knew that planes could fly without power and he was able to land the plane on the Hudson River without the plane braking apart, without hitting a ferry boat and without losing a single passenger. The sales rep, a former Marine told me, "Everyone on the plane was quiet. Not one person panicked. As a Marine, I was trained to focus on one mission at a time. I said my prayers and when we landed I helped people get into the lifeboat." He lifted five people out of the ice-cold water and helped them climb the 12-foot ladder up to the rescue boat. He was second to last to climb on board the boat, with Captain Sullenberger climbing up last.

There are many heroes in this world and as an engaged sales manager, your role is to turn your salespeople into heroes.

Gerhard Gschwandtner - CEO, Selling Power - October, 2015

The Power of ^{2} : Exponential Sales Leadership

Chapter 1: The Challenges of Today's Sales Organization

Great leaders are almost always great simplifiers, who can cut through argument, debate, and doubt to offer a solution everybody can understand.

-General Colin Powell-

The Sales Manager's "Comfy" Position

So here we are: another book on sales. If you are looking for the same old, same old boring corporate talking heads chatter, you may want to just close the cover now. This book is not going to fit into the usual mold. And after reading it, you might not either. So go ahead, but don't say we didn't warn you.

Let's start off by calling a spade a spade. You know your job as a sales leader is oh so easy. (Yeah, right.) Being in a position of leadership in a sales organization is a lot like running a fire drill that never ends in that things are in constant motion and it is easy to get distracted by all the noise and lights.

According to the latest 'thought leaders' all you have to do is generate a winning strategy that will exceed your sales goals. Sounds easy enough, except it's not. In the real world you are doing battle with a multi-headed hydra. You take off one set of snapping teeth and two more rise up in its place.

You are trying to leverage your people, clock in at endless meetings (that flow with the top speed of cold syrup), track performance metrics (and then apply them in a meaningful way), and handle the general tsunami of sales management tasks, phone calls and emails that threaten to swamp your desk every day.

If that all sounds exciting, there's more. In between all of the administrative tasks you have to shoehorn in enough hours to train, mentor and guide and equip your all-important sales team. Because you see, while you are busy managing and containing all of this, you are supposed to well, actually *lead.*

It's all about the L Word: Leadership

Leadership itself is a big topic, one that we will dive more deeply into as we go along. For now, suffice it to say that *managing* is not leading. Forecasting and metrics are not leading. The only thing that is *leading* is…well, leading.

Authentic leadership is tough enough in and of itself, regardless of the field. Leading while in the challenging position of being a sales manager is even harder because of the nature of the field. Besides the busy administrative schedule referenced above, team building represents a massive investment of time (the one commodity that is always in short supply in a sales organization.)

In order to be effective, you have to touch base with team members on a regular basis. This often goes well beyond the required daily meeting where you, as a sales manager, are supposed to cram six hours of information and encouragement into a one hour slot.

When it comes to sales meetings, what you need is a laser focused session that pinpoints a strategy so effective it looks like it was planned by Navy Seals. What you get is usually along the lines of a sales meeting involving some sort of Death by PowerPoint where team members struggle to stay awake and managers pontificate about seemingly meaningless/endless metrics (or become sidetracked by verbal train wrecks that eat up precious minutes).

Why are Real Leaders so Hard to Find?

Sales leaders are in short supply because the talents you need for sales are not necessarily the same ones you need to lead. You see, sales leaders not only need to know how to communicate, they have to understand the material that they are sharing. It is all too easy to hide behind jargon and analytics and then blather on without really saying what team members can use in their real world daily client interactions.

Another reason that sales leaders crash and burn is that companies tend to promote people who excel at selling. The logic goes something like this: Tim consistently exceeds his sales goals. He is goal oriented, driven and competitive. Tim is therefore the ideal candidate to promote into the vacant sales manager position.

Sales do not (Automatically) a Sales Manager Make

The hard truth is, just because someone can sell does not mean that they can manage, much less *lead*, a sales team. Tim may be a juggernaut when it comes to hitting his mark in the field where he has a massive amount of autonomy. His position in a sales leadership role however, draws on different skill sets such as empathy, an ability to motivate, problem solving and time management (where he is also expected to fulfill more administrative and other time dependent or structured duties).

Tim may also lack the emotional intelligence of teamwork. Instead of being the lone wolf in the hunt, Tim must elicit cooperative behavior from a diverse group. In other words, Tim the sales star may not be able to replicate himself because he does not know how to transfer his innate skill set to his team.

And, if he is like most promoted-fresh-from-sales managers, he is likely to be thrown in over his head and then expected to swim like a fish. He may be able to scrape by, dog paddling his way from crisis to crisis, by using metrics like water-wings to keep afloat. Even if Tim is adaptable, new sales managers are also hamstrung by a lack of tools and end up resorting to ever more panicked sales initiatives that does little to enhance long term success.

Of Zebras and Sheep

While the prospects might be challenging, there is some good news, leaders are always in demand. Effective sales managers stand out like a zebra in a field of sheep. They know how to train and deploy their people as well as how to motivate them. (Hint: by motivation we do not mean using a fear based approach, but rather a structure that rewards and motivates improvements in a meaningful way.)

No matter where you look, there are always a lot more followers than there are genuine leaders. And for good reason, the herd mentality is simply all too easy to follow. It takes a great deal of conviction and courage to go against the grain and create from the inside out. It also takes something else, namely character. In order to launch others, you must have the personal traits it takes to build rockets. Then, of course, there are other challenges which we will explore to a greater degree in upcoming chapters.

The Reality of Selling in today's marketplace

Once upon a time selling was a much more straightforward proposition. You made some calls and booked your appointments. You gave a targeted presentation and if you tweaked it to fit them, the client would be likely to buy your service/product. Clients relied more on you for two reasons: first, you were the expert (there was no superhighway of information available 24/7 and you had more innate authority in the eyes of the client) and secondly, they *liked* you. You built up a relationship with them over time, often by wining and dining them.

Now your customers expect more (much, much more). In today's market, potential clients are more informed than ever. Because of this, sales has evolved from a one-sided presentation into a complex collaborative effort that involves the customer. Buyers have access to a broad range of information. They are not just informed, they are *hyper-*

informed. They are demanding too. They know what they want and what they are willing to pay to get it.

If you expect to do business with them, you need to have a unique selling stance that drills down into their world. You must understand their problems and issues. You must have a nuanced value proposition that goes well beyond a one-dimensional sales pitch or tri-fold brochure. In other words, you (and your team) must become a *resource* to them that they can mine for their specific needs.

In short, they expect you to be informed and savvy in a very competitive market. You need to understand not only where they are in the buying cycle, but how to leverage that information.

You are not just competing with other companies; you are vying for the attention of your market in an information soaked, technology laden, media driven feeding frenzy of optimization and value realization that starts long before you first shake your client's hand at a face to face meeting.

The Four Challenges to Creating an Effective Sales Presence (AKA Dominating Your Niche)

As we have already pointed out, the market is in a constant state of flux. New challenges require new approaches and innovative solutions. Your search for answers may lead you far afield as a plethora of self-appointed gurus point to the latest theory of everything regarding sales. While they may differ on the fine points, most will agree on these top challenges:

Changing Markets

The world is changing and so is business and this isn't your daddy's market anymore. From social media to relational selling, there are strong shifts in the marketplace. You have to create an open-ended strategy that allows you to bend with the changes or your company will be just another casualty of the new global market.

In response to the new dynamics, many sales organizations are struggling to adapt. Some are moving away from the traditional sales representative in the field to inside sales where members of the sales team work more from a centralized location utilizing phones and email as their springboard to closing sales. Other organizations are trying different models that aim to deploy their sales resources in a more targeted manner. No matter which structure a given company chooses, it always comes down to being able to create targeted offerings that build revenue and retention.

Buying and selling cycles are also an important factor in a company's sales success or failure. As we have already pointed out, buyers are more informed than ever. Make no mistake, information really is power. At one time, salespeople were at the helm, until new technologies forever changed the sales landscape by empowering buyers with knowledge and truly global options. The buyer is now firmly planted in the driver's seat and the seller is more and more just along for the ride.

Clients live in what we like to call the popcorn age where they demand instant access to solutions faster than you can pop a bag of Orville's finest kernels in the breakroom microwave. It is less and less about the buying cycle and more and more about the organic way that companies operate and have a need to buy. Customers express an interest, evaluate and then decide to purchase based on their perception of their needs, not yours (although your sales engagement does play a key role).

Sales Education and Training is another challenge that we have touched on, but there is a lot more that could be said. In fact, whole books could easily be dedicated to this one subject alone. The main problem that we see with training is that it is often built from the top down rather than the bottom up. By that we mean that it is not necessarily geared to the needs of the sales staff. To be blunt: it is not designed with the learner in mind. Sales team members are often expected to drink from a firehose rather than receiving training that supports actual learning and comprehension.

Training is also used like a club in that when sales drop, management leaps into action by adding training that may or may not be relevant. It is rather like throwing paint on a wall because there is a leak. You can cover it up, but it isn't going to solve the underlying issue. It is going to leak again the next time it rains. This again goes back to sales managers that do not really grasp the nuances of the analytics they are using to gauge performance.

Additionally, training cannot be applied on a hit and run basis. You have to permeate the sales team with a clear mission, constant feedback and ongoing reinforcements that help the message sink in. Sales team members must be coached in a meaningful way that allows them to develop and achieve real results. Training has to address an issue and then guide ongoing behavioral changes through feedback and open conversation and learning opportunities which boils back down to implementing thoughtful, authentic leadership.

Building and managing a sales organization

Have you ever watched a movie that just kind of fizzled out? The plot was good, the acting was fine, but somehow it never really got into gear. You may have walked away without really even knowing what it was that failed. All you know is that it left something to be desired, even if you can't quite put your finger on what it was. Sales organizations can be like that too. They may recruit and hire decent sales representatives and yet still never find that secret sauce that takes it to the next level. There can be any number of reasons for this, but in our experience these are the main culprits:

- Sales team members are not given the tools they need to actually sell. They may lack a documented path or support that makes success more likely.

- Sales team members are too unfocused and are not spending the majority of their time interacting with the client.

- The system of rewards is not geared towards the sales reps. Compensation has to be meaningful or it may not create an incentive that aligns with the needs of the team. (This does not always take the form of money, although that is important.) If you simply up the monetary compensation, it does not automatically follow that sales will increase. In fact, your people may actually become more complacent and do just enough to stay in their position.

- Sales metrics must be used like a tool; while you can drive a nail with a screwdriver, using a hammer makes it a whole lot easier. Analytics must make sense. Then, and only then, can they be used in a productive way.

- Experienced sales leaders must be able to translate, transfer and transform their sales team into a well-oiled machine. Translate meaning that they can explain and simplify. Transfer meaning that they can pass skill sets along. Transform meaning that they can motivate and bring out the best in their team.

Complexity of products and services

High tech products and services can create a bewildering array of complexity that did not even exist a decade ago. New products and upgrades to existing products roll out like clockwork on a conveyor belt of ever-changing technology. It seems like what is in today will be obsolete almost as fast as it can be released. From a plethora of financial services, to mobile and computing devices and software, to wearable tech, to choices about which wine to have with dinner (there are over

1,800 kinds of wine available in the US alone), clients in today's world have a veritable mountain of choices.

The buying public not only has a voracious appetite for the next great thing, it has an increasing amount of media fragmentation to learn about them. (Media fragmentation refers to the way customers are informed across various media platforms such as social media like Twitter and Facebook, LinkedIn, mobile apps and websites as well as print and television ads.) And, to make matters even worse, what works on one media platform such as social selling, may fall flat on another.

Training and re-training – product/service and sales technique

All of this means that companies are scrambling to just to keep up. Every time a new product is rolled out or a 2.0 version is released, sales staff have to be trained and retrained. It can be like drinking from a firehose. Researchers have pointed out that learning has its own arc and curve. That being the recency and latency effect in learning. Basically it boils down to our ability as humans to take in, and process, information. We tend to remember something from the first and last of a presentation, but forget the middle (often the more important information) being presented.

When you combine tight deadlines, ever-upgrading tech, disengaged sales staff and poor trainers you basically wind up with a hot mess. Sales trainers do something more akin to information dumping than actual training. This is really shocking since ramping up and onboarding are critical needs in any sales organization.

Ramping up for a rollout requires that all systems are good so that each sales member understands the product, has access to information and training and that the processes are all connected. Yet there is an overwhelmingly disorganized system in most companies that does not prepare sales staff to actually meet the needs of their clients.

That, in turn, leads to more stress, more problems and less and less time to deal with it all. How bad is it? The numbers are abysmal; according to the <u>Harvard Business Review</u> [i]over 30,000 new products are launched every year. Of those, 95%....fail. Much of that failure is linked to ineffective marketing and training. Companies run willy-nilly to crank out a new product without setting up the infrastructure that will support it and then wonder why it crashes and burns.

Lack of Trained Sales People

Besides all of this, there is another dirty little secret in the world of sales that no one wants to talk about. What is it? It is the fact that very few companies want to invest in building (training) actual sales people. Colleges certainly don't teach it and there is often no infrastructure in place in most companies that teach the art of sales. Instead they focus on the product itself and try to hire people that have been in the field for several years. They are getting harder to find.

You see, a few decades ago the really big boys like IBM and others, used to train legions of salespeople and they would later enter the secondary market. These people knew how to sell. They were seasoned veterans. The big boys had invested a lot of time and effort to train them and help them to hone their skills. They had been around the block enough times to know how to overcome objections, how to engage and how to solve problems. Research has shown that most companies today spend the lion's share (70-90 %) of their time teaching their staff about the product, but neglect to actually teach them how to sell it.

Nowadays there is less coaching and mentoring and more "Hurry up and hit your mark or we will find someone else who can". Very few sales managers have themselves been trained. They simply do not have the time, inclination or even the talent (know-how) to coach, mentor and train the people that report to them. Studies have shown over and over that one-shot training sessions simply do not work. Without ongoing support and feedback people just slide back into bad habits.

Creating internal organization distinction, confidence and respect of the sales organization

Success is culture driven. Make no mistake, excellence does not just happen. Like healthy grapes growing on a supported vine, successful companies create a framework that allows them to flourish. They create a consensus and develop a process that is clear and inclusive. By that, we mean that they have open communication, clearly defined goals, systems that can be replicated and a culture that values their people. When team members are treated like people, shown respect and listened to, they perform better because they are happier. Team members are not cattle to be assigned an ear tag and driven into the field. The flip side is also true: happy people who feel valued sell more and create healthier balance sheets.

As in all things, the leadership you have in place sets the tone for the entire sales team. If you *say* it, you have to actually *do* it. For example, if you claim to value your people, you have to invest in them and their welfare. If you say that transparency is a priority, it has to be lived out. And what's more, organizational structure is critical because it shapes and reinforces the culture. Who you report to and how it is done matters. The way hierarchy is structured is going to affect the way that people and process perform. Team building and communication is also built on the kind of organizational structure that is put into place.

Chapter 2: Organizational Leadership (Pros and Cons)

When all you have is a hammer, the whole world begins to look like a nail.
-Unknown-

Think big...really big...as in large enough to be seen from space! Think Great Pyramid of Giza big. The pyramids represent some of the greatest architectural achievements of the ancient world. Even today, thousands of years later, we don't really know how the ancient builders managed to do everything they so obviously did. To date we have not even been able to duplicate the mortar they used - although we have been able to determine its basic components.

Somehow, they managed to cut, move and stack over 2,300,000 stone blocks - some weighing as much as fifty tons. Using primitive tools, ingenuity and teamwork, they placed these massive stone blocks so precisely that it would have been nearly impossible to insert even a flat sheet of paper into the polished casing stones that once covered the outer surface.

While we could spend literally hours talking about the incredible engineering of the ancients, suffice to say that the achievement is truly worthy of the word 'epic'. At this point you may be asking yourself what this has to do with selling more of your companies' goods and services. Everything.

You see, just as the ancient Egyptians made amazing use of their human resources, modern companies must embrace some form of organizational structure if they are to survive, much less grow and actually thrive. While your company may have less to do with erecting monumental edifices and more to do with the bottom line, the principle still applies.

Organizational Structure- More than a Pyramid Scheme

Every company needs some form of overarching organizational structure in order to maximize their market position. Without a plan to *organize, motivate and lead* your team, you are more likely to end up with a pile of rubble than something that will last beyond your next profit and loss statement- much less stand up to the ages.

This, of course, begs the question, is there an ideal organizational structure? Not really. Although there are certainly proponents of one kind over another, each one has both pros and cons. Organizational systems can range from ad hoc systems thrown together based on the natural evolution of a small company, to well-planned systems that run as tight as a German train schedule.

While a detailed analysis of every conceivable organizational structure is beyond the scope of this book, the next section contains a brief explanation of the basic organizational systems, as well as some of the pros and cons of each.

Flat or Horizontal Organizational Structure

A flat, or horizontal organizational structure, is quite common in smaller sales organizations. It is really rather simple, basically, a flat structure means that there are fewer layers of management.

On the plus side of a flat organization, employees usually have more autonomy, allowing for greater flexibility and responsiveness to customer needs. Instead of hunting down a member of management to make every decision, salespeople have some leeway in taking ownership of their sales activities and latitude in management of customer issues. Customers' needs tend to be taken care of faster. This can result in a better overall customer experience.

On the other hand, while the small company atmosphere can promote unity, a feeling of camaraderie or team spirit, it can also create a situation where some sales staff perceives that there is favoritism. Salespeople may also feel that they have limited opportunities for growth. Because of this, they may become less engaged.

Other pitfalls to a flat structure include the problem of scalability. While horizontal structures can work well in mom and pop sized sales organizations or smaller departments, it is extremely difficult to scale up in larger companies, departments and or divisions when certain roles have to be replicated or 'cloned' over and over again.

Hurry up and Wait

Even though some of the decision-making process in a flat structure can be faster, inconsistencies may occur when companies begin to expand. This occurs because each executive becomes responsible for more and more staff members. Flat organizational structures can therefore lead to job confusion, questions about the chain of command and the aforementioned feelings of favoritism. Whether there is favoritism or not, esprit de corps is affected if the sales force *perceives* it to be one way or another.

Moreover, because all of the people within a given department are likely to report to a single sales manager, managers can easily lose touch with their sales people and end up falling back on familiar tools such as metrics and sales numbers rather than truly managing, much *less leading* and training their sales staff.

This is especially true if no one has implemented a repeatable sales process that sales team members can use over and over. Without guidelines, a formula for success and strong authentic leadership, sales teams can lose their focus. Team members may feel that they have been left to drift in an ocean of uncertainty. They may even be hesitant to speak up, ask questions or seek solutions because of those perceptions.

Instead, sales team members believe that they have to sink or swim on their own. (More often than not, there is a lot of the former, rather than the latter.) Of course, this is not just a problem with flat organizational structures, but it can become quite apparent when there is a looser organizational structure with fewer insulating layers of management.

Tiered Organizational Structure

Another common organizational structure is known as a tiered structure. Tiered organizations, also called "tall" or "vertical" structures, may be based on customer size, customer opportunity or industry specific. Tall or tiered organizations, although organized in many different ways, simply add more tiers, or layers, between the upper management and the sales team members.

You can think of a vertical organizational structure as a massive "Dagwood" style sandwich. The layers of bread, condiments, cold-cuts of meat, lettuce and tomatoes are all stacked high.

The CEO is like the olive on top with layer after layer of bread (middle management), team members, divisions and sales personnel all filling up the plate.

The enormous toothpick that holds them all together is the hierarchy (chain of command) and culture of the company itself. One of the biggest problems with this type of structure is that it often leads to a lot of finger pointing, passing the buck and shifting blame. Like a Harry Potter style vanishing cloak, larger numbers provide a certain herd mentality of anonymity.

Furthermore, there is a real danger of creating redundant systems that hamper real effectiveness. In such cases, the proverbial left hand does not know what the right hand is up to. In order to avoid wasting resources, managers really have to be on their toes, paying close attention and communicating well with both team members and other department heads.

This may mean creating a mandatory schedule of meetings that can hamper productivity due to time constraints. Metrics and numbers once again become the focal point. Let us be clear, the danger is not that a given department or company will use some form of analytics to measure progress, but that numbers alone do not necessarily convey real-word trends.

Information is power only to the extent that it is understood and leveraged into actionable goals.

Numbers can become more important than *actual* leadership and true management. Additionally, although more management layers do provide more control, responsiveness can suffer because the grapevine is longer. Or because employees feel pressured to report to more managers who may give conflicting directions. Employees may feel that their loyalty is tested or be confused by an unclear chain of command, and not know who to listen to when instructions are not clearly defined. As you can see, communication problems can easily arise, hampering the decision making process and in turn, altering the customer's perception of their experience.

Organizational Structure Grouped by Customer Size: Grouping Pros and Cons

As we have already touched on, there are many ways to structure a sales organization. Another common structure that is of a hybrid of the tall and flat systems that is organized by grouping or divisional structure. This is frequently seen in companies that create territories or geographic regions in which customers are grouped according to opportunity, location and or potential customer base numbers. Another frequently used form of organizing is based on the number of salespeople/employees or even the needs or size of the client organization. One prospect for instance, might have 1000 employees, but represent little incremental revenue because they don't need the company's product or service whereas another, smaller client, may offer a larger sales opportunity because they do have a critical or ongoing need for a given product or service.

Organizational grouping can also be based on a customer/prospect industry (trucking, telecommunications, IT, staffing, manufacturing, healthcare, etc.) or product sales (where the salespeople are knowledgeable about a specific product, services or line). On the plus side, organizational structures that are grouped by customer or account size can allow salespeople to become extremely familiar with a given market and or customer-specific information.

Clients get the needed attention because sales reps develop a feel for the overall spending/buying patterns. They can leverage information and contacts and make the sale based on where the customer is in the buying cycle. Dedicated accounts can make clients feel that they are important and this may promote more loyalty. This is frequently seen in the famous "80/20 rule" where a few key accounts are at the heart of company sales numbers.

Employees may also perceive that they have more lateral and vertical advancement opportunities because of the divided territory structure. Allowing people to grow into positions by giving them upward movement can create better retention rates.

The Cons

Contra wise, customers/clients of a grouped structure, might begin to feel that they are dealing with a bureaucracy- depending on how well their individual accounts are being managed. Additionally, this model may not serve smaller customers (who can represent a hefty chunk of corporate revenue). Smaller accounts may be overlooked in favor of the "big boys" that are perceived as more important to the company wellbeing.

Here again, the critical message that many companies seem to forget: to succeed, any company must find a way to treat all customers, regardless of size, with the same commitment to service.

Remember, you are never just selling a product or service. You are selling a solution. As Theodore Levitt famously quipped, "People don't want to buy a quarter-inch drill; they want to buy a quarter-inch hole." And just because you hit the ball out of the park yesterday, you still have to meet your client's needs and expectations tomorrow.

Hunting the Elusive, Wild Unicorn of Customer Care

Regardless of the structure, all companies must create a perception of value in their customer base. In other words, they have to provide genuine customer service. Customer service, it seems, is a lot like hunting unicorns. You tend to hear a lot about it, but it is rather scarce in real life. Customers and prospects need to feel that you "get" their problem. You can talk about customer service all day long, but you have to put some boots on it every day to make it work. In other words, walk your walk the way you talk your talk. Treat all customers equitably or move over because someone else will, and there goes your edge.

Besides, purchasing behaviors vary over time and today's big fish in the pond may be tomorrow's minnows and vice versa. Some companies put all of the resources into the proverbial egg basket, which means company fortunes are staked on the shifting fortunes of customers.

Proudly Promoted

Another issue (also not limited to any particular organizational structure) is the tendency to promote great sales people from within. Moving high sales achievers sounds like a no-brainer. Because all good salespeople are automatically great managers. (Ri-ight.)

That's like saying that a good fisherman is automatically a great ship's captain. Casting a net and steering the ship require two separate skill sets. Many companies make this mistake and then wonder why they are not meeting expectations and goals.

Of course, solid sales people can be strong leaders, but it does not follow with the same certainty that the sun will rise every morning. Just because someone can sell or knows a given product, it does not follow that they can lead people, or will do well in another territory, with another product line or an executive position.

Inappropriately promoting high sales achievers in a flat organizational structure can lead to managers that become fixated on critical numbers, leading them to overlook crucial relationships (and team building opportunities with their sales staff).

Sales executives, especially those who are not natural born leaders, may become overwhelmed, overstressed and end up hiding behind metrics, passing the blame and applying undue pressure onto team members for not meeting quotas.

Forget London Bridge: Morale is Falling Down

It is a lot like the old joke that the floggings will continue until moral improves. In an atmosphere of fear, team members are likely to become increasingly dissatisfied and begin to hunt for greener pastures. You see this a lot in sales organizations such as car dealerships.

Sales professionals often cringe at the mention of used car salesmen, but the stereotype persists for a reason. Check out the online job boards for a week or two. You will see the same sales jobs posted over and over. Each one will promise a hefty training rate of pay, bonuses and benefits to lure in more and more sales staff to replace the last sales staff that left due to the pressures of the position.

You could argue that it is the nature of sales. True. Sales can be a hard horse to saddle, much less ride, but many times the problem lies not with the nature of the animal, but with the way the rodeo is managed. No matter how you organize your particular sales force, what really matters is how you **manage** it. Or **lead** it. (Or fail to manage it.) Simply adding more bells and whistles (in the form of kick-off meetings, bonus programs, contests and giveaways of vacation packages to remote island destinations) may work to some degree but will not necessarily fix the real issues that are lowering productivity.

Assuming that you really have built a better mousetrap (and your product rocks like a Rolling Stones concert), if your numbers are waffling, it may not be your compensation structure that is at fault. It just may be that your people are fundamentally not happy, well trained or mentored, or utilized properly.

Here is a hard truth: if your salespeople are not shiny, happy people, your customers will pick up on it too. Soon your numbers will tank and you will find yourself bleeding red ink all over your profit and loss statements. Like a row of dominos throwing off the balance, each problem tips the balance and entire systems can become less effective.

Silos and Hoarding

Another big issue, perhaps one of the most critical of all, is a problem known as "silos". In the business world, silos refer not to grain silos, such as are used in farming, but to autonomous structures created within companies. Like children on a playground refusing to share their toys, silos mean that managers and employees alike are hoarding information and protecting what they perceive as their territory.

They reduce productivity by duplicating efforts and blocking effective communication. Instead of working together, managers, teams, individuals and divisions are either in competition, with each one worried about covering their own...(ahem), *assets*. Once again, it comes down to leadership, or a lack of it.

Numbers Matter, But People Matter More

No one would ever say that metrics don't matter. They do. Without sales goals, quotas and numbers, nothing happens. As business author Peter Drucker is famous for saying, "What gets measured gets managed." If there is no accountability, no finish line, there is no way to know if you are winning or losing the race.

Having said that though, sales executives can be inundated by a forest of data (and overlook growing the actual sales tree). Metrics alone, without understanding the abstract and nuanced business realities that undergird them are next to useless. Data for the sake of data garners you almost zilch. To properly use metrics, you have to be able to leverage the information in a meaningful way.

As Laurence J. Peter, author of "The Peter Principle", put it, "Some problems are so complex that you have to be highly intelligent and well informed just to be undecided about them."

It is a lot like a doctor telling someone with a headache to merely 'take an aspirin and call me in the morning' rather than digging deeper to diagnose what the real medical issue is. Let us be blunt here: to really lead people, you have to actually care about more than just the process.

Real leaders give a damn. They demonstrate it by the way they invest in the people. The process matters, as do the numbers, but people: real flesh and blood human beings, matter more.

A Lesson from Band of Brothers

In sales, as in life, it is always about the underlying relationships. Great leaders know this. They do not just yell, stomp and demand that people hit their mark. You may recall a gripping miniseries based on the book by Stephen E. Ambrose called "Band of Brothers". (If you have not seen it, you probably should.) Set in WWII, the true story follows the exploits of E Company, aka, "Easy Company" of the 2nd Battalion, 506th Infantry Regiment that was assigned to the famous 101st Airborne Division of the US Army.

As the story unfolds, Easy Company carries out one daring mission after another. These truly heroic men risked everything to battle their way across Europe in a series of brutal skirmishes, fighting against battled-hardened German units.

Originally trained at Camp Toccoa in Georgia, the men at first struggled under the leadership of First Lieutenant Herbert Sobel. Sobel pushed his men hard, focusing on maintaining strict discipline and military precision in a very rigid and inflexible manner. He seemed to be more concerned with discipline for the sake of discipline, rather than the well-being of his men.

His leadership is so poor that at one point, many of his non-commissioned officers attempt to resign all at once. Following a confrontation with his executive officer, Sobel is transferred to another location and does not land in Normandy with his former troops.

Real Life Heroes

After the commander of Easy Company is killed in action, the real-life hero of the story, Lieutenant Winters, is forced to assume command. He promptly leads a recon team of 12 men against entrenched German troops with a row of 105 mm howitzers sprouting like monstrous teeth from a series of trenches just three miles south of Utah Beach.

After considering his options, he deploys his men in such a way that they are able to disable the guns, meet up with Company D reinforcements and even retrieve a German map, (with detailed intelligence), that is later proven to be invaluable for the Allied troops landing on the beaches of Normandy.

The individual heroics of the men under fire is unforgettable, as is the example of Lieutenant Winters who was largely responsible for the easier landing of the Allied Forces at Utah Beach. He was later awarded the Distinguished Service Cross for his actions (and was recommended for the Medal of Honor). Sadly, due to a bureaucratic snafu, he never received the much deserved Medal of Honor.

The point in sharing this true story, apart from the fact that it highlights the bravery of our armed forces, is the idea that Winters, having trained with the men, was able to rise to great heights because of his ability to fight alongside of his men, rather than simply dictating their actions from above.

Lieutenant Sobel focused almost solely on spit and polish, tight marching formations and crisp uniforms (metrics) rather than leadership (genuine management). Lieutenant Winters, on the other hand, was able to lead from within. He exposed himself to danger and led by example rather than ruling by fiat.

That one difference probably saved the lives of hundreds of brave soldiers struggling up the bloody beach under enemy fire. Even though, let us hope, your salespeople are not literally going to war, they still need genuine, flexible and knowledgeable leaders that can come alongside of them and fight the good fight to create lasting benefits for all concerned.

The Good, the Bad, and the Rotten

As demonstrated by the above story, a poor manager just cracks the whip louder, dangles a juicy carrot, or resorts to using some form of stick to punish stragglers. Good leaders come alongside of their people; they guide them and help them improve their aim with meaningful, thoughtful feedback.

That is not to say it is easy; in fact, it may be easier to herd cats than it is to help team members build a lasting formula for success. Analytics and metrics alone do not a sales manager make. Having the data does not mean that you know how to make use of it (draw insights from it or leverage it into actionable plans) or that your sales managers will use it as a tool to build a cohesive sales team.

Bottom line: without the proper management, sales managers may begin to resemble (dare we say it?) taskmasters a la the pyramids. Threats and harsh criticism may have worked with the ancient builders, but that form of motivation is short sighted and in the end, will not serve you well in the long run. The only thing that you will build is your blood pressure, ulcers and lower rates of job satisfaction.

Chapter 3: Introducing the Engaged Sales Management Squared Method (ESM²)

You manage things; you lead people. — *Rear Admiral Grace Murray Hopper*

Much like the overused words 'customer service', the term leadership gets tossed around a lot these days. You read about it everywhere. Inspirational quotes and sound bites from "thought leaders" are read aloud at sales meetings. Books, videos and programs crowd the shelves, promising the latest and greatest ways to succeed in business.

From one moment to another, there are probably half a dozen different sales leadership gurus expounding the virtues of using this stick or that carrot. While in reality, real leadership seems to be about as common as sense.

So why is this book any different? Why should you pay attention to us when so many other voices are clamoring for your time and attention? Because what we are proposing is not some flavor-of-the-month, three easy steps to team building exercise in futility. We are talking about a workable, sustainable system built on a deep understanding of human nature and sales—real-world dynamics—if you will.

In this chapter, we will begin to look at the ESM² method in more detail. For now, you only need to understand the basic building blocks. Briefly, the basic components of an Engaged Sales Management Team include:

· Management is present at every level of the sales process sales team member focus on sales lead generation and prepping customers using a solution oriented approach to value propositions
· Sales managers assist with the sale and meet with clients

- Metrics are analyzed separately to determine the effectiveness of the process

Mentoring Vs. Coaching

If we could sum up the difference between engaged sales management and other forms of leadership it would be more like mentoring than coaching. Coaches may be on the same team, but they wear a different uniform than the players. Coaches guide from the sidelines, shouting out instructions while the players move the ball up and down the field.

We are not talking about telling. We are talking about doing—coming alongside your sales team and working with them to meet common goals. This is a new playbook. And yes, there is a hierarchy, there are metrics, but they are *tools*, a means to an end, not an end in and of themselves.

Where to Start

Now, you may feel that all of this sounds great, but where will you find the time? Let's be blunt here, we are all busy. Life is a juggling act already in progress. Successful people do not have more time than anyone else. As Zig Zigler quipped, "Lack of direction, not lack of time, is the problem. We all have twenty-four hour days."

Whether you are the President of the United States or a bus driver, everyone gets the same amount of time in a day. It is not how much time you do or don't have. It is what you do with it that matters. It is a matter of establishing priorities. What can wait? What needs your attention now? Only you can determine that.

It comes down to having the foresight, and the will, to implement and follow through with a plan. Make no mistake, this is a real commitment. Most things that are worth having require some effort. No one ever climbed Everest and said, "Wow. That was simple."

This is an investment in yourself, your goals and most of all, your people. Yes. It will cost you. If you have been using the traditional 'top down' strategies, this is going to seem strange at first. Most people don't like change and this may initially be an uphill climb.

The payoff, however, is very real. If implemented thoughtfully, the benefits of the Engaged Sales Management Strategy include better retention of trained sales staff. With proper mentoring and support, team members can thrive. They feel valued. Let's face it: happy sales people are not going to be trolling for more work. That means lower turnover, less time spent training and more sales. Everyone wins.

Metrics become a tool instead of a weapon. 'Nuff said. Customers benefit because sales people are happier and more attuned to their needs. All of this means increased profits, growth and sustainability. It also creates a culture of success, leading to more success.

As Ken Blanchard put it, "The key to successful leadership today is influence, not authority." In order to gain something meaningful, to co-create, you must influence and motivate your people in an entirely new way. It requires a change in the way you think, act and bring people together.

Now for the hard part. Like well-worn rabbit trails, changing hearts and minds can be tough at first. It is easy to talk the talk, it is the walking part that gets a bit tricky for most of us. Doing so though, can increase your sales, your metrics and, last but not least, the satisfaction of building something real. Okay, so much for the locker room speeches. Let's move into the mechanics of putting all of this into motion in the real world of hardscrabble sales.

Lining up Your Ducks

So where do you begin? First, you need to find your bearings. Next, make the commitment to engage your sales staff in as many direct prospect opportunities as possible. In other words, *you* need to get involved in the sales process. Why? Because it not only provides you the opportunity to mentor and groom your salespeople, it also increases the likelihood of closing on the prospective new business. Isn't closing new business the outcome sales managers use as the metric that defines success? YES!

Does this mean that the sales staff is any less capable? No! Will they fail to perform because of your example? Absolutely not! By stepping in and working beside them, the team becomes more capable. Each member benefits from the mentoring, becoming better salespeople.

Real Leadership Creates Leaders

Think about it. The job of sales management is not to produce by force, coercion or the latest slick gimmick. The role of a sales manager is that of a farmer. No one stands over the fields and yells 'Grow!' expecting anything to thrive. Instead, a good farmer scatters seed, waters, weeds and works with the land to help the tender plants thrive. By highlighting what is possible, leaders shine a light onto a better future. Genuine leadership compels others to follow, to move upward and become leaders themselves. A rising tide floats all boats.

Seeing is Believing

Your sales team gets to observe, in real-life sales situations, how to meet customer needs, build relationships and close deals. Team members begin to pull together, modeling the skills and capability of the best and brightest. What better way to learn?

Before you can do all that though, you need to get your bearings. You may need to dig a bit here. You need to take an honest assessment of where you really are. Here's the kicker though, to get to the real truth, the nitty-gritty details, you and your management team, are going to have to check your ego at the office door.

This is not just an exercise in navel gazing or a suggestion box mentality (that will gain you zero traction in the real world). Take it seriously and follow through with your results. You will see change as soon as you begin to be the change. Also, it is worth mentioning here that you really need to make sure your team knows that your involvement is NOT punitive or some sort of interrogation.

They need to be comfortable that your involvement is *not* a negative comment on their capability - it is you bringing your sales skills, your real world experience, your management and leadership into the sales arena to create a greater contribution to the overall success of the organization.

The sales staff is also going to become highly engaged. They have a responsibility to appropriately prepare and qualify the prospect. You will be asking them to prepare the prospect for your interaction. (More about this later.)

Basically, at this point, you need to ensure they understand that they are free to speak about issues so that they can be addressed and corrected. Just as an aside, step carefully here. This is not a free-for-all where team members can ambush each other. Ax grinding does not contribute to the health of any company. You are not trying to create schism and divide people or turn them into tattletales seeking to curry favor or gain retribution for perceived slights and ills.

Instead, this is a real opportunity to focus the group, ferret out real issues and address them openly. You may need to take team members aside so that no one feels singled out and deal with issues one-on-one. Once again, this is often easier said than done. Remember, the goal is to identify and remove barriers that are getting in the way of your people doing their job.

People are not going to want tell you the truth, and you will not be able to remove roadblocks if they are afraid of reprisals. So ask them. Ask them honestly, without hanging the "Sword of Damocles" above their heads, how you can help them move ahead. Find out what works and what doesn't.

Ask and then listen—really listen—to what your people are saying. Then take all of it, the good, the bad, the unflattering and the chest-busting truth and winnow it. Search out the solutions that will serve the entire team. You have to create a win-win situation here. The idea is to create an engaged leadership that grows a cohesive unit.

Most sales managers have been taught that it is all about beating the 'other guy'. It is more of a "Give 'em hell, damn the torpedoes, full speed ahead" mentality based on competition and one upping the other team. Of course, you have to swim with the sharks, of course, you have to hit your mark, but there are a ways to win that benefit everyone.

Cooperation goes a lot further, creates authentic leadership, and spawns more success than Darwinian competition does. You have to build an 'esprit de corps' that will support teamwork:

- You work as a team
- You succeed (or fail) as a team
- You plan, improve and correct course, as a team
- You celebrate as a team
- You compensate, reward and recognize, as a team

The upshot of this is the creation of a cohesive unit fully capable of getting the job done. Team members learn from one another, support one another and become less prone to hoarding knowledge and skills that could improve the dynamics within the group.

It fosters a sense of group pride, camaraderie and problem solving. People can pull together and get more done. Handled correctly, salespeople come to view success based on outcomes instead of ego.

Sales Lead generation

Sales lead generation is another one of those eternally hot topics. From social media and networking to digital marketing, sales contacts are grist for the sales mill. The great thing here is that with the Engaged Sales model, your team can focus on growing their contacts, cultivating relationships and solving customer problems.

Solution Oriented

If you think about it, sales is all about solving problems for customers. You identify a need, or in some cases, create one by clever marketing that creates a desire. Once the need is present, you proceed to educate the client in such a way as to express how your product or service provides a solution or benefits them in some way. In other words, you create value for the customer by 'feeling their pain.' A sales transaction is a journey with defined segments that include:

· Asking questions (research)
· Listening to the responses and identifying with their problem or pain
· Informing (educating) the customer on how your product meets their needs
· Qualifying them
· Closing and finalizing the sale

At each point, the sales representative and the customer work together to define the problem and then agree on the solution. Keep in mind that sales alone cannot be just be the end goal of customer contacts. Rather, sales are a by-product that naturally comes as a result of the broader relationship.

The customer experience not that of the company, or salesperson, is what matters in the end. Good sales people understand their role as a facilitator and are able to connect with the customer at a level that builds trust. The real goal is to fulfill a need or offer a genuine solution to a client's problem. Easier said than done though isn't it? It is natural to put your needs before those of your customer. For long-term success though, hitting your sales numbers has to be a process.

Sales process involving the manager

Speaking of which, here is where we talk about transforming your sales managers into sales enablers. To do that you will need to shift the responsibilities of the administrative duties and metrics to a third party. Of course, metrics matter. You have to have someone who keeps an eye the analytics. The sales manager must have some means of judging performance and metrics certainly play a part in that.

Overall performance metrics need to be created, analyzed and parsed out in easily digestible chunks that allow the sales manager to grasp them at a glance. Ideally, an administrative arm of the sales organization should do this. This allows the sales manager to focus on being in the trenches with the sales force while still drawing conclusions, making changes and enhancing team productivity.

Does that remove the sales manager from accountability? Absolutely not. In fact, having a sales manager that is intimately involved enables them to more fully comprehend the sales dynamics behind the numbers.

Draw Better Conclusions and Implement Powerful Changes

The sales manager becomes more empowered to draw conclusions and steer the process while building teamwork. He or she has been on the ground, involved in prospect qualification, prospect preparation up to and including closing the sale. The sales manager rises or falls with his or her team. Because of this, when conclusions are drawn and the changes are made, team members are more likely to accept criticism, coaching and mentoring.

Besides the obvious benefits of leading from the inside, reassigning the metrics and administrative support, sales managers no longer have to waste valuable time gathering information, cross-checking its validity, analyzing and drawing conclusions based solely on data that may or may not be skewed.

The value of personal involvement and experience with the sales team in the field is priceless. Instead of using valuable time to keep up with all of the day-to-day minutiae of administration, the sales manager is closing deals in the field and making appropriate changes within the context of team and customer needs.

Here is a quick breakdown of the process thus far:

- Focus on building honest relationships and solving customer problems
- The sales team is a team. Period.
- Sales staff focus on leads and qualifying prospects
- Change the sales manager role from administration to senior sales support who comes into the sales process to assist with closing as needed
- Create an administrative/ analytics arm of the organization that can present/ dispense information in bite sized chunks

Is any of this easy? Not on your life! No one ever succeeded in making an omelet without breaking a few shells. The point is to move past your comfort zone, reach into the unknown and adapt as you move forward with your team.

Chapter 4: (ESM²) Benefits to the Sales Staff

Never lonely: The Missing "i" in Team

If you have ever played any kind of sports, you have heard a speech about the infamous "i" that got left out of the word "team". We think we know where that missing vowel is hiding: it's in the word "ignored". You can also find that elusive letter hiding in words like "isolated" and "incomplete" and sadly, the "i" is all too often snuggled up right next to the word "incompetent". (Ouch.)

Look, there are times when things are tough to hear and this is one of those times. There are some really good sales programs out there, but many companies have sales managers that only clock in to smack people down. Leaving your team dangling in the wind like sales piñatas (taking all the hits from unresolved product, customer support or program issues) without providing authentic tools and a creating a genuine team effort (allowing everyone to work as a unit), is a form of management incompetence that quite frankly, costs in more ways than one.

The proverbial left hand needs to understand what the right hand is out there doing or both will be empty.

The upshot is that sales team members can feel like they are always responsible for screw ups but never given the support need they to succeed. No one wants to get called on the carpet and they may respond by becoming busier (but less effective). They may also lose confidence and panic, rushing from one lead to another instead of really investing in any of them. (And that is *if* they stay at all. They may take the first exit ramp out of there, but more on that subject later.)

Is Fear Really a Good Motivator?

Some sales managers are under the impression that stress and fear are good things. The old school mindset is that sales is about being a shark slicing thru the murky waters, ready to compete and eat everyone else for lunch. The truth is that fear motivates only enough to make people hit the bare minimum. It motivates them only for the short term and makes them that much more likely to coast along as they seek out greener pastures.

Besides which, fear has a few cousins that it likes to hang out with, namely divisiveness and selfishness. When people are afraid they naturally want to protect their own interests. That means that they build walls, hoard information and basically seek to cover their own rear ends. They may point fingers, sidestep blame, and basically subvert the organizational structure and culture of a company.

Toxic leadership uses fear, locker room sales speeches, emotional outbursts, and threats to maintain order and enforce their will. But creating a climate of fear simply does not produce long term corporate benefits. And frankly, they show a lack of both character and leadership skills.

Weak minded people use fear and intimidation. Autocrats use control systems built on unhealthy competition and maladjusted methods centered on manipulative behavior. And when they do, the whole system can grind to a halt.

Fear stifles our thinking and actions. It creates indecisiveness that results in stagnation. I have known talented people who procrastinate indefinitely rather than risk failure. Lost opportunities cause erosion of confidence, and the downward spiral begins. — Charles Stanely

As it is, unsupported team members may feel the pressure mounting so they become more and more stressed. When people are stressed out, especially over a period of time, they really can't bring their "A" game. Instead they become territorial, defensive and divisive.

Everyone starts pointing fingers and trying to dodge the bullet of responsibility. Productivity can plummet even though your sales people seem busier than ever. Each presentation becomes a make it or break it moment with more and more of the latter and less of the former.

Show Up and Throw Up

Expecting an under prepared sales person to exhibit a consultative, solution oriented sales approach is likely to result in a "show up and throw up" sales presentation. When lacking the proper skills, the "sales presentation" turns into a feature and benefit regurgitation without regard to whether the service or product meets a prospect need. It becomes a verbal brochure review and we assure it does not produce quality results. In fact, if a sale does result from such an interaction, there is no way it becomes a lasting relationship because the purchase is uninformed with no guidance on how to use the service or product…so it is destined to fail in the long run.

In the Engaged Sales Management approach, we ask the front line sales member to focus on prospecting and qualifying activity. By doing so, we focus their skills on identifying the client needs, business problems and fostering a strong relationship. The skills involving matching products and services, conveying such to the client, overcoming objections and closing become a shared activity with the sales manager.

We will say it again: the best method to finding out if the customer actually *has* a particular problem and *needs* your specific solution by actively listening to them.

The most basic of all human needs is the need to understand and be understood. The best way to understand people is to listen to them. — Ralph Nichols

Sales numbers come naturally when you are **actually focused on improving your customer's world**. Learn how to improve your team's ability to hear (and understand the meaning behind what is being said) and your sales will increase organically. This means more than just waiting for a break in the conversation so they can fill it up with the facts and figures and rote answers that they learned last week in a "training meeting". This leads us to our next point, to teach your people *how to fish*.

Experiential Learning: Hear One, See One, Do One

Before we break down our method, let's back the sales bus up here for a moment and touch on something we covered earlier: that is the complexity of products and services and the sheer volume of material that sales team members encounter during a given week or month.

As noted, products, buying cycles and technologies are always changing, making it incredibly difficult to stay informed while still meeting individual sales goals. In large part the difficulty lies not only in the amount of information, but that which is transmitted, accepted and retained. The potential information overload, in turn, has something to do with a little thing known as the learning curve.

What is the Learning Curve?

Over a century ago a scholar by the name of Hermann Ebbinghaus developed a theory known as the learning curve (referring to the relationship between time and memory). Basically it states that during a learning experience (such as a lecture) a person's ability to absorb is set to 100% on the first day. On the second day, the rate has dropped to somewhere between fifty to eighty percent. From there it falls to somewhere between two to three percent at the end of a thirty day span.

How can a person retain, much less use, what they do not even absorb in the first place?

Tell me and I may forget; teach me and I may remember. Involve me and I may learn. — Benjamin Franklin

So how can you improve the learning curve? Well, in medical schools they have a process known as "See one, do one, teach one." It really refers to active learning in which skill based concepts are applied and practiced in real life situations. In relation to sales, it means that team members are mentored and taught (see) a skill set in the real world and then encouraged to use (do) what they have seen.

Learning then moves naturally from rote presentations to solution oriented thinking, allowing the team members to adapt what they have learned and apply it in new scenarios. It takes some of the pressure off because they become more comfortable with the information. Once they "own it" they can spend time focusing on what the customer is actually saying (active listening) and then respond in an appropriate way that is more likely to create long-term customer satisfaction and sales.

In this new environment and sales management structure, how should we expect the sales team members to respond? If we believe the popular literature regarding employee satisfaction, engagement and expectations, the employee wants to feel respected, supported, important and reasonably compensated, in that order. Thus, employees want managers that exhibit respect and support of their team.

As we explained in chapter three, the most supportive manager behavior possible occurs when you (the sales manager) are striving alongside them to gain the sale. And, as sales productivity increases, the ability to compensate the sales rep climbs as well. Increased success for the company creates a corresponding benefit to the employee. As for the question above, it answers itself. Sales team members thrive because they see the benefits of the process, the company as a whole benefits accordingly.

Experiential Training in a Nutshell

The benefits of experiential learning cannot be stressed enough. A recent study presented in 2012 by *Training Industry Quarterly* demonstrated that mentoring led to an increase of transferred skills as knowledge at a level almost double that of other traditional methods. Experiential learning accelerates the ability to absorb, retain and use information. Replacing learning by repetition with learning through experience accomplishes the following:

- Bridges the gaps between theory and the real world of sales
- Lowers stress by creating a safe learning environment geared to the individual (leading to better retention of sales staff members and lower staff turnover costs)
- Prepares the sales member's mindset for long term success by creating effective sales habits
- Dramatically increases sales engagement levels (creating happier customers)
- Allows for dramatically increased levels of retention of information
- Allows for better assessments of training effectiveness (sales team members can demonstrate their level of understanding)
- Creates an exceptional return on training investments

A New Way to Gauge Success

In our system success is defined as the ability to qualify the lead. This creates an environment and sales process where asking questions is more important than perfecting the pitch. — Jay Blakey

In the Engaged Sales System, the focus of each team member is to qualify the lead. *They are not penalized for failing to close.* Instead, in our system the sales team member focuses almost exclusively on qualifying the sale. Now that may seem to be a radical departure from the norm because, well, it is.

The Basics of How it Works

It begins in much the same way as a traditional sales funnel. The sales representative ferrets out suspects or potential customers. Once they confirm the customer's interest, the customer becomes a prospect. The sales team member then begins to groom the sale by learning the degree of interest and need and learns where the prospect is in their buying cycle (readiness to buy). At the appropriate time (you), the sales manager is then brought in to tag team and close the sale. *The sales manager role is to work in tandem with the sales representative to reach the same sales goal.*

The result is more freedom for the sales representative to focus on their responsibilities (prospecting, active listening and problem solving for the benefit of the prospect). They feel less pressured and stressed and can therefore function more effectively.

The Engaged Sales Model:

- Lowers stress and increases confidence (leading to increased sales staff retention and better field performance)
- Builds better relationships (between team members and in customer relations)
- Encourages on the job training
- Replicates itself by building skilled salespeople that then become sales leaders
- Increases sales and long-range customer satisfaction
- Increases the sense of teamwork as each person focuses on certain areas and works towards a shared goal

The beauty of the experiential learning model, applied to Engaged Sales Management, is the rate of sales skill development of the sales team. As they are exposed to the techniques, thought processes, presentation skills, and ability to overcome objections by the you the sales manager *in multiple real, actual sales scenarios,* the progression is truly exponential!

Imagine the value of the "teachable moment" with the sales rep when, immediately after the prospect interaction, you as the sales manager, can engage the rep in a discussion of what went right, what went wrong or why he/she did this or that - especially when that discussion is taking place after the prospect has answered with a great big YES to becoming a customer. Celebrating and learning all wrapped up in one package that benefits every player. Now that, is how you make a team.

Chapter 5: Benefits to the Prospect/ Client

Let's not sugarcoat this. There are probably dozens of other companies out there who have a similar product or service to yours. How are you going to sell more and do more with that much competition? How do you stand out like a sparkly disco dancer in a room full of people doing the waltz?

You change it up so that everyone is dancing to a different tune. To do that you need to change the process from selling to *consulting* and change the focus from your product to focus *on the way the client experiences the process.*

This is very different from what we like to call the 'car lot experience'. The car lot experience is a *perception*, on the part of the prospect, that they must face a scripted, standard sales process that is applied to each and every interested prospect, without taking their needs and wants into consideration. Much like a rat in a maze, they must submit to unnecessary steps if they wish to reach the cheese (i.e. Purchase a car). Now, if you are in the business of selling cars you may not like this image very much, but studies have shown this is the overall *perception* of how it works in the mind of the car buying public. It does not matter if this perception is even accurate. What matters is how they perceive it and how they feel about it. (In sales, the buyer's perception *is* reality.)

And in this case, potential car buyers dislike the way cars are sold. For instance, in one study conducted by Edmunds.com (a site dedicated to identifying car buying trends), people stated that they hate car shopping so much that they would—get this—rather give up sex for an entire month than haggle with a salesperson over the price of a car.

Participants also indicated that they were willing to forgo participating in social media or using their smartphones for 30 days if it meant being able to avoid the back and forth car buying sales process. Overall, participants in the study rated the car buying process as being less appealing than a visit to the DMV and filing their taxes!

What exactly makes the process of buying a car so much like running a marathon? The answer is in the perception of having to endure a one-sided sales process. As Andy Rudin (the managing principal of Outside Technologies, a company dedicated to B2B sales) once quipped, "People do not dislike sales people, they dislike bad selling." And it's true: clients are interested not in being sold to, but in being understood.

Ixnay on the 'Carlot Experience': Giving an Opportunity to Express

No matter who they are, be they suspects, prospects or clients, people are first and foremost human beings. And as such, they want to be listened to and understood. That is why our system is people focused. In the Engaged Sales Model the client is the star and the process, utilizing the sales team and the manager is the answer.

Not the presentation, and certainly not your sales numbers. In our process the prospect gets to explain and express their specific needs. It should be noted that the qualifying process changes in that the salesperson does not follow the normal back and forth in which the customer expresses objections or concerns and the salesperson responds with something to overcome their objections. Instead—and this is really important—**the prospect gets to fully express their business concern, facilitated by the salesperson without being interrupted with a sales solution to every issue immediately upon expressing it.**

Most people think "selling" is the same as "talking". But the most effective salespeople know that listening is the most important part of their job. – Roy Bartell

This is empowering for both the prospect and the salesperson and creates a cooperative mindset. No one is preached to, no 'show up and throw up' (which does not work), just an organic process of creating workable solutions specific to the potential client. What better customer is there than the one who understands that they have been part of the solution to their unique problem?

This is the matrix, the very heart of the Engaged Sales Process. Consultative sales uses the natural momentum of engagement to accelerate the sales, without forcing it. This is why more and more companies are moving to the solution based or consultative selling system. The Engaged Sales Process takes it a step further by utilizing the sales team in defined roles to assure success.

We assure you, there is no better, more lasting client relationship than the one who believes they were integral to creating their own solution using your products, services and consultation. Performed correctly, the new client of the Engaged Sales Process not only knows what they bought and why they bought but most importantly, how what they bought solves their business problem.

Perception of Importance

Have you ever noticed how the big boys like Coca Cola and AT&T craft their commercials? Coca Cola for instance does not focus so much on the taste of their fizzy sugary drink. Instead they show scenes of happy people who feel good. All of their advertising focuses on the basic human desire to fit in, to be accepted and to feel good about themselves.

Why? Because it works. People respond to it because we all have an innate need to be noticed and feel good about ourselves. Why do people want to wear or have trendy brand name items? Why do they want to drive a fancy car or live in upscale, exclusive neighborhoods? Why do wealthy people want to make large donations and have their name plastered on buildings? Because it makes them feel good in some way.

Our process builds on the need to feel important. It creates that sense of importance in the mind of the prospect because it is innately flattering.

The selling organization deems them to be so important in fact, that they warrant the special attention of the next level in the organization (the involvement of you, the sales manager). Their problem is big enough, important enough to send out a call for you as the sales manager to show up to help them in person.

Perception of a Consultative Sales Process: Know Your Stuff

Why do businesses hire consultants? To solve problems and provide expertize. Consultants are in demand because they are often able to provide 'hacks' or shortcuts that can save the client time or money or both. Consultants can provide a framework for change too. A consultant is able to see many sides to a problem and use their experience to point to a solution. We believe that this consultative role is one that good sales leaders can capitalize on by seeking to become a resource rather than simply seeking to make a sale.

This again goes back to having a mindset geared towards actually benefiting the company or person you are selling to. As a sales manager you probably already know a significant amount about your product and market. We would encourage you to go even further and seek to become an expert in your niche and then pass that same passion on to your team members.

Be the Resource

Why? Because adding depth and breadth to your understanding of your industry transforms you into a touchstone for the very people you are selling to. For example, let's say that there are two hypothetical butchers at a local store. One of the butchers cuts the meat and packages it. He is pleasant enough and seems to do a good job. He has it all laid out in front of you. If you ask him a question he will give you a general answer.

The second butcher does all of the above, but he knows every single cut of meat. He knows recipes, cooking times and temperatures, and can explain why one kind of meat is better than another. He is passionate about what he does and it shows. He not only sells meat, he consults with his clients to create meals. His expertise includes helping his clients learn how to use his product.

Now, which butcher would you rather interact with? More than likely you are going to go with the second butcher *because he adds value*. In the same way, you must become so familiar with not just the pros of your product, but the cons too. You need to understand the latest ideas and trends in your field. You should be a learning machine and live this out in front of your team.

By becoming an expert and gaining an underlying understanding of their world, you become more than a sales presentation. The customer begins to respect you, changing their perception of the experience from sales oriented to genuinely consultative in nature.

Breaking the Sales Mold

How do you move ahead and make more sales? How do you beat everyone else at the game? By creating a game that is rigged in the customer's favor (and therefore yours). In short, you overcome the competition by *doing it better, smarter, faster, more completely and with more consultation.*

You focus not on drive by sales hits, but upon creating a path to excellence that includes meeting your client's underlying needs. That is how you close and create *lasting* sales. And that is how you motivate your team. So instead of allowing your people to grow soft and decreasing their motivation, Engaged Selling actually increases it and makes the process more profitable and enjoyable for everyone concerned, including and especially for the customer.

Chapter 6: Benefits to the Sales Organization

True story: a guy goes to an estate sale and buys a handcrafted, heavy walnut chest for a measly $100. When he goes to unload it, he turns it on its side and hears something rattling inside that sounds like a slot machine paying out. Which, as it turns out, was not too far from the truth; the chest contained a long forgotten secret drawer that was quietly covering up a small fortune in rare coins, gold bullion and highly collectable gold jewelry.

Why are we telling you this?

Because sometimes the answer you need is secreted away in plain sight. (And the rewards can be unexpectedly huge.) In the Engaged Sales model for instance, a few key changes can unlock hidden benefits such as better staff retention (due to lowered stress levels), increased productivity, higher closing rates and an overall healthier bottom line. We will take a look at each of these areas in turn before we give an explanation of how you can implement our model, thus allowing you to begin reaping substantial rewards for yourself and your sales organization.

Lowered Operating Costs

First and foremost, one of the biggest potential benefits comes in the form of lowered sales costs. According to *Business News Daily*, aside from the cost of materials and manufacturing, the biggest expenses in a given sales organization are tied to payroll and marketing[ii]. At roughly 70% of your operating costs, your workforce in and of itself represents a massive investment worth protecting.

Losing key sales team players, for instance, increases those costs exponentially. Let's be open and honest here: sales burnout and turnover is a real (and costly) part of every sales organization. Between the immediate disruptions (and resulting missed sales opportunities) to the ongoing expenditure of time and resources to locate a suitable replacement, to training/onboarding them to the actual recoup timeline for your company to cover those upfront costs, you are probably looking at somewhere between 12 to 18 months just to break even.

Keep Calm and Sell

In the meantime, your sales are probably going to drop as you attempt to find the right key for the sales lock. For example, let's assume that you lose one of your mid-range producers due to promotion, a lateral move or simple sales burnout. In our hypothetical case, your lost sales team member, while not in the top sales performance slot, still hits his or her sales quota on a regular basis. You take on a likely candidate and begin the long process of onboarding them.

Even on day one, they cost you simply by showing up for training. The cost of their ramp up continues to grow well into the first few months of their employment. If, for some reason, you have landed a candidate that is not suitable and they either leave or are terminated before they begin the long climb to becoming a profitable investment, your company stands to lose a massive chunk of revenue.

How much? Well, according to the *Sales Effectiveness Study 2011-2012* conducted by Depaul University, the average turnover rate in a given sales organization is around 28%. And the average cost of replacing them is around 20% of their annual income, which breaks down to a whopping $114, 957, depending on the overall salary of the sales team member [iii]. How can you decrease this? By creating happier team members. Happier sales reps means better sales numbers and higher levels of retention. **An effective sales leader in the Engaged Sales model leads to better sales team members and therefore lower potential costs of turnover!**

Juggling Less and Doing it Better

In a typical organization members of the sales team are focused on closing sales while juggling a myriad of related tasks such as prospecting and qualifying. In our system, team members share the load with yourself, the sales manager, in a tag team approach that frees them up and makes everyone happier and more productive. It also has another unexpected benefit, in that your sales team members will begin to experience a dramatically increased closing ratio.

Why? Because of those listening skills we pointed out earlier. As you probably know, there is an old dictum in direct marketing called the 40/40/20 rule. It was presented in the 1960's by none other than direct marketing guru Ed Mayer. He believed that in direct sales marketing, 40% of your sales closings are due to the target audience. Another 40% can be credited to the perceived value of your product or service and the final 20% was due to your ability to be creative and get their attention.

This applies to your sales reps in the field in that they increase the attention and engagement of the prospect not by having a slick ad campaign or direct marketing mail out, but because they are genuinely interested in the client and what the client has to say.

So much so that closing rates begin to climb even when they are simply qualifying the prospect. In which case, the sales team member does not need to wait - if the customer wants to place an order; they can just go ahead and make the sale. They don't need to wait for your presence and instead should be empowered enough to negotiate "on the fly" (instead of telling the prospect that someone else will have to get back to them in order to answer a question or meet an objection).

Increased "Spontaneous" Closings

A sales leader spending time in the field with the sales team will rub off on them. Team members are going to become empowered as the sales leader models the process in front of them. In this way you will organically create one of the most powerful and sought after solutions in any industry: the ability to replicate success.

Additionally, spending more time in the field alongside team members allows the sales manager to see them in action. Just as 'iron sharpens iron' the leader will be able to help hone their team members' skills. Furthermore, you will be able to build a more complete and accurate portrait of how they spend their time, where they focus and how smoothly they handle client relationships.

In Summation

By partnering with your team you will not only be able to mentor and grow your sales team, but to place them more strategically. If one member of your team excels in one area, they may be ideal for a related area or better suited to head in a more focused direction. Additionally, you will be able to more effectively weed out those who just can't cut the mustard. The value of this can't really be overstated as in reality a poor performing employee is costly on many levels. This is especially true of new hires, because adding a poor performer to your sales team costs you an estimated 30% of their yearly salary.

Top performers on the other hand show as much as a 67% variance in their productivity (over that of other sales team members). They not only generate more revenue but tend to increase the productivity and raise the morale of other team members. There is an old saying that a "rising tide lifts all boats" and it is certainly true in the world of sales. So as you work more closely with your team, you will naturally discover more about them.

As we have pointed out, this hits directly to the root of the burnout and turnover problem. In many companies high turnover is a massive problem that refuses to die. Our system tackles the problem head on by lowering stress and providing the ability to succeed. Simply put, it allows others to follow a recipe for consistent results and provides a road-map that allows them to reap clear rewards for their efforts.

You will learn what works and what doesn't for each team member. You will be able to motivate them in a way that fits into their strengths and goals. They become transformed because you share the load as a team. As mentioned, not everyone is motivated by the same things. Some people crave recognition as much or more than they do financial awards. Study after study has demonstrated that team members want to feel respected, supported, important and reasonably compensated- in that order.

Grow Your Own Leaders

Team members also want to know that they have the opportunity to create something that they can not only take pride in, but can grow with. Our path builds a clear progression that is easy to identify. As their sales tenure builds, they will become more and more successful at prospecting and qualifying. Their skills will improve and they will learn to present the material in a more natural way.

They will experience and live the sales and closing process so often that they are likely to evolve into higher sales positions and management roles. Or they will perform themselves out of the organization, which is entirely possible, yet not necessarily a bad thing, because with so many coming up in the ranks, you are still likely to retain superior sales team members.

And the ones that do stay will be more qualified to lead authentically *because they have seen it done. They've grown into the role as a sales leader as a natural byproduct of the system.* Our model actually grooms and nurtures future sales leaders. It plants seeds and cultivates success through teamwork and mentoring. It really is a form of servant leadership that builds a more satisfying team environment. Loyalty is not demanded, it is earned.

Releasing the pressure may seem counterintuitive, but it actually increases productivity for each sales team member. Increased closing ratios also means that they do not have to meet with as many overall prospects. The cost of operations in the sales department will fall and you will likely not need as many team members even though you are now achieving (and maybe even surpassing) your sales quota objectives.

Better Client Relations

Additionally, more qualified prospects means happier clients too. We believe that this is due, in part at least, to the fact that the entire process promotes communication that it truly is more consultative in nature. Customers feel more informed because they are participating in a process that is geared to ferret out their real needs and thereby solve their problems more effectively.

This also aids in client retention because clients feel more engaged, more informed and therefore more confident in their purchases. Their overall sales experience is going to be more enjoyable and that translates to long-term client relationships with fewer sales team members required to keep it running.

You Still Need a Great Product

There is, however, one rather large caveat that needs to be stated here: while your sales team members are likely to start pumping out better numbers like a wildcat oilfield gusher, if your product support and customer experience does not match up in the long run, you are going to fall flat. It all goes back to building a better mousetrap in the first place.

As long as your product is stellar and the ongoing support structure such as customer service, technical support and other ancillary functions are present and accounted for, you will see increased sales across the board. If, on the other hand, your product falls flat and fails to meet the customer's real-world requirements, all of the sales expertise in the world is not going to work.

No one wants a broken mousetrap and they will naturally drop you like a steaming hot potato. Assuming that you have your ducks lined up, quacking in unison and ready to roll, your organization can expect to grow.

Overall, our method allows you to: seed new sales relationships by relentlessly qualifying them, increase revenue using a leaner, meaner sales model, grow and retain your best, cull out the chaff and lower your costs, all while reducing headaches and improving morale all around.

Chapter 7: Things to do to Convert to ESM[2]

Have you ever made a New Year's Resolution? If so, how did that go? Did you actually manage to hit any of your goals? Did you lose that last ten pounds or change whatever it is you promised yourself to change? If so, good for you. You certainly hit a home run because, statistically speaking, only 8% of the people who make a resolution manage to keep it.

If not, welcome to the 92% club. It's that way in business too isn't it? Big ideas come rolling down and everyone is supposed to jump on board and implement the changes. Sometimes it goes over like a cool glass of lemonade on a blazing hot summer day. Other times, the results are more like the dried husk of the lemon, sans cool glass of anything.

The reason? Change is an act of will as much as anything else. Much like a captain using all his might to turn the wheel of his ship away from an iceberg, change requires strong leadership with a heck of a lot of intestinal fortitude to boot. Unless you want your company to stay in the 92% club, you need to be invested in the change so much that it becomes embedded in the very fabric of the corporate mindset. It must permeate the organization and honestly lived from the inside out or else it is useless. In short, it takes a sincere commitment backed up by action.

And let's speak plainly here, although it can be extremely rewarding on many levels, transitioning to the Engaged Sales Model can be challenging. So you are going to need the ability to follow through when the waters get choppy.

Depending on the size of your organization and structure, you may even have to dismantle and rebuild some sections of your business. If, for example, your current sales organization utilizes the sales manager position as more of an administrator (focused on metrics, classroom training, product knowledge, issuing orders to staff, etc.), you have big changes to make to organizational structure (and likely to key personnel as well if you are going to successfully implement this model).

Where to Begin

Like any good sailor will tell you, it all starts with figuring out where you are in the first place. To do that, you will need to get your bearings by taking a ruthless assessment of where you are (and possibly take a hard look at how you got there.) Not in the sense of pointing fingers and laying blame, but in an attempt to understand the reasons behind the way things are functioning.

You will have to be committed to a sincere, unvarnished evaluation of the sales manager position as an authentic leader. And you have to ask the critical question of whether or not your managers are, in fact, you're most seasoned among your sales professionals. Do they have the ability to coach? Will they be able to mentor? Can they close sales in the field? And do they have the capacity to imprint that pattern on other sales team members?

Additionally, here are some of the other questions that you need consider:

- Does the sales manager position exist to serve management or to serve the needs of the clients?
- Are you ready to accept the client feedback you receive from the Engaged Sales Manager position?
- Are you ready to allow the sales manager role to become Engaged (and create the sales operations function to support the Engaged Manager)?
- When revenue begins to grow as a result of the Engaged process, are you ready to compensate the sales team for the exponential growth?

- Can you create a fair assessment of the existing sales manager (be it yourself or someone in that role) staff to determine who fits the Engaged Manager profile? (Can you find the "Major Winters" within your current sales managers?)
- Are you ready to reassign and/or eliminate those that don't exhibit the necessary attributes?

We would strongly recommend that you ask these questions (and any others you deem relevant), before you begin to transition. While you are doing so, you will also want to clearly articulate your intentions to team members.

After answering any relevant questions outlining your intentions and expectations, you will also need to act quickly and actually implement the required changes. Be advised that this may cut your staff down considerably, either because you have seen a need to pare away dead wood, or because some make the choice to leave rather than perform at a higher level.

In all honesty, if you explain the benefits, most of your team members will want to remain. After all, they can look forward to greater earnings, less stress and more rewards in the form of better communication, teamwork, and mutual respect. As an aside here, do not overlook the need for team members to feel valued.

People want, often more than they desire monetary rewards, to be acknowledged and validated. Which is why we have tried, in this short volume, to encourage a certain view of what leadership really is: *servanthood based direction.* We have shown that our model is based on leadership characteristics just as much as it is on a structural form. Besides being organized differently with a few key changes, our system rests on four less tangible pillars. These being:

- Building a culture of success through leadership that engages
- Mutual respect and teamwork

- Offering genuine value propositions to clients by becoming a resource
- Modeling/mentoring successful closings and seeding future leaders for ongoing success

Even if you take nothing else away from this book, we hope that you will remember those four core values. We believe that even just changing those aspects of your business, will bring you greater levels of success as well as create happier team members and clients.

Moving Things Around

Now back to the organizational side, if you are fully committed to leveraging our model, you will need to free up your people so that they can function in their new and expanded roles. First and foremost, as a sales manager, you need to be able to work alongside the team.

Training and development must go hand in hand. It must be ongoing, Upcoming sales leaders must also be groomed and promoted based not only on their ability to close, but their power to lead. True leadership is a rather rare commodity, therefore it should be highly valued, nurtured and sought after. It must also be remembered that this is not a popularity contest or political back office pandering where the good old boys club reigns.

A leadership position has to be earned in the field then put into action every day. Additionally an in-depth qualification process should be in place with clearly stated rungs up the ladder so that team members know and understand how they can advance. Our model can be scaled up and down to fit within a larger organizational framework by restructuring and moving certain key responsibilities in order to free you up in the key position of sales manager.

Instead of being shut into a room reading endless reports, the sales manager role shifts to become a hands-on sales role. This cannot happen if you are bogged down by mundane (yet important) administrative tasks. If you want them in the field, mentoring and closing, you are going to have to create an ancillary team member that handles things such as metrics and analytics and other administrative tasks. This team member needs to be partnered with you, the sales manager.

Create a Separate Analytics or Sales Administrator Position

We like to designate this team member as the Sales Administrator. You as the sales manager, will need to hand off the duties of collecting and interpreting all of the metrics to the sales administrator. We must emphasize again that while it may seem that we have been somewhat critical of metrics, it is only in the sense that the sales manager role should be focused on sales and sales alone.

Metrics are critical to the success of any sales organization, however the *interpretation* of metrics is extremely time consuming and needs to be assigned to someone who can focus their full attention to that area. By doing this, you are freed up to *act* on the metrics.

These two roles work not in competition, but rather in full cooperation with one another. You could go so far to say that the sales is the right hand while analytics/metrics are the left. It must also be pointed out that while certain attributes make a wonderful sales leader, they are rarely the same as those that create a good metrics analyst.

Studies have shown that as a rule, sales and people skills are a more right-brained activity whereas those who are left brain dominant tend to perform better in crunching numbers, analyzing data and interpreting complex sales patterns. There is often some degree of overlap, however these two functions require very different skill sets. That is why breaking them up into separate roles makes sense on multiple levels.

It is also our assertion that the valuable feedback provided by metrics is often overlooked or misinterpreted by sales managers. This is often not because they are not capable (although some admittedly are not), but because their attention is too divided. They simply have too many irons in the fire to process everything and still manage the daily administrative tasks along with tracking, training and managing a sales team. There is an old adage about being a jack of all trades and yet a master of none: that applies here.

If anything, metrics become even more valuable in the Engaged Sales Process for two important reasons:

1. The metrics associated with field activity are a *direct* and relevant reflection of the individual contributions of the members (prospecting and qualifying for the sales staff), closing with the manager. If anything, metrics become more valid in our model.

2. The metrics associated with revenue production are a direct reflection of the TEAM contributions.

Commitment to TEAM selling

The Engaged Sales Model will also shake things up in a different way in that sales team members are no longer going to spend the majority of their time alone. Instead they will be expected to function as a part of a group. Whereas they would be more likely to be a lone wolf, they must now run with a pack and frankly, some would rather not. They may be quite comfortable prospecting, qualifying and closing. They may neither have the inclination nor the skill set it takes to shift gears when required and to work as a cohesive unit.

To which we say, "If you can't change the people, *change* the people." There is nothing, we repeat, nothing that will shoot a hole through the side of your sales ship like team members who do not play well with others. If you are building a team everyone has to communicate and work together, supporting one another. The lone wolf mentality (which is sometimes coupled with a high ego) needs to work for the benefit of the team, not against it.

If they are not willing to step *up*, they may need to step *out*. Having said that, we hasten to add this, you will need to exercise some good judgement here. Obviously, you are not going to want to cut them loose if they have a proven track record or are otherwise stellar salespeople. That would be like throwing the baby out with the bathwater. Instead we would encourage you to hang onto proven talent. You may only need to **deploy** them differently in order to get the most out of them.

If for example, your organization has multiple products/services and/or a unique marketplace, it may be possible to develop a standalone sales force for these high performing individuals. This is especially true if they are in fact consistently high performers. The critical thing here is not to mix and match. Don't try to squeeze a round peg into a square hole by shoving non-social team members into a team where you know they are just going to create friction.

Instead, try to leverage their performance abilities by assigning them to a specific set of customers or selling a specific set of services or products. Once they are assigned, make sure to manage them within the highest level of the organization. That way you still utilize their talents without destroying the fabric of the team mindset you are building.

Only you can make this call. You will know if you can use them in the broader context of a team or if you need to set them apart so that you leverage their abilities in a more focused role. If they are not fit for special deployment in a standalone role and do not seem to be able to mesh with the team, then you will have to consider other options. Some may be able to transition to other roles, provided that they have the temperament and skill sets you need.

During this winnowing process, it is entirely possible that you may experience a short term reduction in sales. This is to be expected and is, in our experience, nothing to panic over. However you should be aware of it up front and plan ahead. Assuming that you have prepared well (and have at least 50% retention of staff as a result of transition), incremental sales in the Engaged Process should make up for any gap or short term drop in sales activity during the transition in fairly short order.

Commitment of Marketing Support

Additionally, in order to take full advantage of our model, you will also need to ensure that there is collateral marketing support. By that we mean the commitment of marketing support- materials that have been developed to follow the Engaged Process. This assures that there is marketing support for the Prospecting, Qualifying, Presentation, and Closing Steps (i.e. general literature that explains the products/services and creates intrigue in the mind of the Prospect).

Remember that the consultative sales process is more complicated in some respects because it is less of a transactional process and geared more towards solving a given problem *to which the client does not know the answer.*

Standard materials will really not help in this case. Having a slick PowerPoint presentation is nice, but it may not get you past the front door. Instead the focus of your material must show value based on how the product or service solves the client's problem and meets their need. Marketing materials should also help to minimize the risk in the mind of the client.

Case studies can be very effective in this regard as they reassure the client by addressing hidden anxiety. They create the perception in the mind of the client that the path to implementation can be a successful one (and that is not going to restrict or disrupt their workflow).

These materials should include:

- Q&A materials
- Relevant case studies
- FAQs
- Prospect interview material for use in qualifying
- The value proposition
- Objection identification
- Competitive contrast for Presentation

Structured Compensation

Another component of the Engaged Sales Model is that of structured compensation that supports the new version of the organization. It goes back to living, dying or thriving as a team. You rise as a team. You succeed as a team and you share the rewards as a team. Everyone benefits from the process. In order for our sales model to gain you the most traction, it has to be mutually beneficial at all levels. This is something we must stress because some management levels may not understand the underlying idea. They may view it as some pyramid scheme that involves what they consider "double paying" incentive compensation. This is simply not true and needs to be understood from the get-go. It is more like allowing the work horses to graze the field they are plowing by reaping the rewards of the team success.

The first step is to make sure executive management understands the Engaged process and is comfortable that sales staff may in many instances be involved to prospect and qualify, leaving presentation and closing to the manager. We hope that we have provided you with ample evidence that this is a GOOD thing. From the standpoint of finance, you will need to secure upper management's agreement and support to do two things:

1. A total budgeted amount of new, incremental revenue

2. A percentage of the new, incremental revenue allocated to incentive compensation

Once those figures are established, determine the percentage of total allocated incentive compensation that will be available to the sales staff and the manager. Assign a smaller percentage of the sales staff incentive comp to meeting or exceeding the goal metrics of number of prospects identified and number of qualification client meetings.

Assign a larger percentage to closing meetings and closes. The manager's incentive comp should be apportioned in a similar manner - a small percentage associated with sales staff metrics and the bulk to actual new incremental revenue production. Depending on your organization, the Engaged Sales Team may have a component of compensation (base plus incentives) tied to revenue retention.

We would caution you here however, that retention related comp should be a small percentage in order to guard against distracting sales team focus from new sales. If the client is happy with the delivery of products and service, this should ensure client retention. A measurement needs to be tied to customer retention so that team members can see and understand a real assessment of the customer base and how keeping it healthy impacts compensation.

If competition is heavy, maybe an account management function is applicable but it is not warranted just to shoulder the sales organization with existing client relationship management. The idea is to ensure an effective compensation plan that rewards retention and encourages top-line growth in the process. We believe that Engaged Sales Management can create a healthier bottom line for the organization while allowing every participant, from prospect to sales rep to upper management, to prosper and succeed at higher and higher levels.

About ProActivate

ProActivate is a forward thinking company that provides highly qualified sales talent to companies around the world. ProActivate is not just another staffing company using the same old, same old traditional recruiting methods. ProActivate uses the latest in behavioral quantification and simulation evaluations to spot the best possible fit for your winning sales team. The loss of a top tier sales rep can literally cost an organization a million dollars or more (in the form of lost revenue, ramp up time, resources and missed sales opportunities).

We can help you protect your revenue by partnering with you to effectively and efficiently fill the gaps with strategic hires. For more information about how ProActivate can take your team to the next level, contact us today email: sales@proactivate.net

www.ProActivate.net

References

[i] Harvard Business Review
http://hbswk.hbs.edu/item/6496.html?wknews=02142011

[ii] Business News Daily http://www.businessnewsdaily.com/682-3-big-expenses-your-small-business-can-cut-today.html

[iii] Effectiveness Survey
http://www.salesleadershipcenter.com/pdf/2011-2012-Sales-Effectiveness-Survey-ppt.pdf

.